territories

territories

niki landau

Territories
first published 2007 by
Scirocco Drama
An imprint of J. Gordon Shillingford Publishing Inc.
© 2007 Niki Landau

Cover design by Terry Gallagher/Doowah Design Inc.
Author photo by Paul Lampert
Printed and bound in Canada

We acknowledge the financial support of the Manitoba Arts Council, The Canada Council for the Arts and the Government of Canada through the Book Publishing Industry Development Program (BPIDP) for our publishing program.

Production inquiries should be addressed to:
Theatre PANIK
info@theatrepanik.ca

Library and Archives Canada Cataloguing in Publication

Landau, Niki
    Territories / Niki Landau.

A play.
ISBN 978-1-897289-25-9

    I. Title.

PS8623.A513T47 2007   C81'.6   C2007-904870-6

J. Gordon Shillingford Publishing
P.O. Box 86, RPO Corydon Avenue, Winnipeg, MB Canada R3M 3S3

To Paul

Niki Landau

Territories marks Niki Landau's playwriting debut. She is Artistic Co-Director of Toronto's Theatre PANIK and has acted across Canada and the United States. Her performance credits include George F. Walker's *Suburban Motel* cycle, as well as Jason Sherman's *After the Orchard* and *Reading Hebron*. *Territories* won the 2005 SummerWorks Festival prize for Best Production and was a finalist for the Dora Mavor Moore Award in the Outstanding New Play category. Niki's latest play, *The Corpse Bride*, is part of Nightwood Theatre's 2007 Groundswell Festival.

Production History

The first full-length public performance of *Territories* was produced by Theatre PANIK and Theatre Passe Muraille in 2005, with the following cast:

SARA: .... Niki Landau
HISHAM: .... Sam Khalilieh

Director: Paul Lampert
Set & Costume Design: Teresa Przybylski
Lighting Design: Bonnie Beecher
Sound Design: John Gzowski
Stage Manager: Andrea Shurman
Assistant Director: Robert Levine

The first public performance of *Territories* (abridged version) was part of the 2005 SummerWorks Festival, Toronto, and was produced by Theatre PANIK with the following cast:

SARA: .... Niki Landau
HISHAM: .... Sam Khalilieh

Director: Paul Lampert
Set & Costume Design: Teresa Przybylski
Lighting Design: Bonnie Beecher
Sound Design: John Gzowski
Staged Manager: Jessie Shearer
Assistant Director: Robert Levine
Assistant Stage Manager: Nellwyn Lampert

Characters

SARA: .... A Canadian Jewish woman
HISHAM: .... A Palestinian man from the West Bank

Note: The play begins as a solo show. The program for the play reads: *"Territories: A Monologue"*, and lists Sara as the only character.

As lights are going down, sounds of a tennis match...

VOICE: *("Wimbledon" style.)* Quiet please. Quiet please.

A match strikes in the dark. Two Shabbat candles are lit. SARA sings the traditional Hebrew prayer over the candles.

SARA: *(Sings.)* Baruch ata adonai
eloheinu melech ha'olam
asher kidshanu bimitzvotav v'tzivanu
l'hadlikner l'hadlikner
shel yom ha-kippurim.

She stands for a moment in silence. In the following monologue, and throughout her solo show, SARA speaks to the audience and to Marnie. She refers to Marnie as if Marnie is in the room with her.

I have no idea how long I've been standing in the dark when she walks into the room and says, "Happy Birthday girl" and I say *(Looks at clock.)*, "Nineteen minutes. I've got nineteen minutes, don't rush me." She holds out a box and I say, "I don't want it. You should have been here hours ago. "At least open it," she says. "I carried it on my lap the whole way." "I don't need to open it, Marn, I know what's inside."

It's a Loblaws cake, white on white with purple icing, and on the top is written, 'Marnie and Sara Turn Thirty.' *(Beat.)* She smiles. *(Beat.)* "It's Yom Kippur, Marn."

She puts down the box, puts her feet up on my new

coffee-table and says, "Only you and I would have our thirtieth birthdays on the day of fasting and repentance." I say, "What do you care? You never believed in fasting." And she says, "So what? You never believed in repentance."

Beat. To audience.

Which is not true.

I make a motion for Marnie to take her feet *(motions.)* off my new coffee-table. She stands up and says, "Jesus, Sara, have you always been this anal or is it only since Alan left?"

Beat.

The repentance comment is bothering me.

"Marn, do you remember Rabbi Bergman making us line up in grade five?"

To audience.

She does.

Every Yom Kippur, Rabbi Bergman made all the kids in Hebrew School line up and ask each other for forgiveness. The Rabbi said the rule in Judaism is you have to ask once, then twice, and if on the third time the person still doesn't forgive you, then God forgives you. Little Tommy Fisher used to ask everybody three times fast. *(Fast.)* "Will you forgive me, will you forgive me, will you forgive me?" And then he'd smile, and flick them on the forehead. I kept telling him, "God is omniscient. He's not going to write your name in the Book of Life if you keep flicking people on the forehead." *(Beat.)* He didn't seem worried.

(To Marnie.) "What?" Marnie used to make fun of me because I was so intense. In grade six, she nicknamed me 'The Jew'. Fifty little Jewish kids,

and my nickname was 'The Jew'. *(To Marnie intense.)* "That's my point. That's exactly my point. I believed in everything. God, the Book of Life, the State of Israel. Everything." *(To audience.)* I can't remember what that point pertains to, but I feel like I won the argument so I say, "Can we get started, please?"

> *HISHAM sits in the audience and speaks in Arabic, 'sotto voce'.*

HISHAM: (Yes, please.)

SARA: Marnie goes to the window and looks out. "What do you believe in now, Sara?" She asks. "Hey. I moved here, didn't I?" *(To audience.)* I'm referring to my very recent move to Israel. No one expected it, least of all me.

HISHAM: *(Not so 'sotto voce'.)* (So the Canadian woman moves to Israel.)

SARA: Marnie picks up a letter that's sitting on one of the many unpacked boxes scattered around the room. It's from my grandmother, my bubie. She wrote it just before she died. The letter says she's leaving the house in Israel to me, as the only grandchild. It says, 'For you, zees maidela, so that you will always have a place to go.' "I see," Marnie says. "You believe in security."

HISHAM: (Excuse me.)

SARA: Security?

> *HISHAM stands and delivers, entirely in Arabic, overlapping SARA's speech.*

HISHAM: (Maybe I could tell you about my security problems. I waited at the checkpoint for six hours in the middle of the day and when I finally got to the front the boy, he looked at me and said, "No more passes today." I had a flight, this is my ticket

(Pulls out ticket and waves it.) ... You will not look at it? Well, good then, fine. Nobody cares. Fine.)

SARA: "Of course," Marnie says. "Ever since you lost the house, you're terrified..."

She is unable to continue.

He exits the theatre. Pause, as SARA regroups before she continues with her show.

(To audience.) "The point is," Marnie says, very emphatically, "now that your bubie is dead, you have no particular connection to Israel. You're only here because your life is screwed up, and you should come home." My god, it's like talking to my mother. *(To Marnie.)* "Maybe you don't remember, Marn, but I met my first love in Israel." *(Beat.)* Marnie says I can't call it love because I was only eight years old. I met him at my bubie's tennis club in Tel Aviv. My bubie always said tennis was a good way to meet boys. "But let them win," she'd say. "Men have very delicate egos, Sara. So it's your choice: Win, or get married." So on this one day we show up and I'm scheduled to play against an Arab boy. It was part of this thing—this community building thing, little Jewish boys and girls playing little Arab boys and girls. I remember walking out onto the court to shake his hand. He was all in tennis whites and so scrawny, barely the size of his racquet, and I thought, Bubie, how am I going to let him win so he'll marry me? And just as our hands touched, someone stood up in the bleachers and yelled, "*(In Hebrew.)* 'Kill him!' Kill him! Don't let the dirty Arab win!" And I started to pull my hand away but he wouldn't let me. He just held on and smiled—

HISHAM re-enters from the balcony, calling out in Arabic, then English, from the audience, overlapping SARA's following speech.

HISHAM: (Excuse me.) Excuse me. Hello. I have a question. Do the candles represent Israel as the 'light unto nations'? Do you equate your need for security with taking someone else's home? Why do you speak to me if you don't want me to speak back? All these people—they are nice, yes, they are very Canadian, but it is like they are watching television. *(To audience.)* Why do you come here? Hmm?

SARA: My bubie was so worried about me playing against the Arab boy that she said she couldn't watch the game... She was sure that something bad was going to happen to me...I said, "Bubie what did you think? He was going to attack me with his tennis racquet?"... *(Beat. She is unable to continue.)* I'm sorry, sir. Excuse me... Sir, this is no way to behave in a theatre—

HISHAM: Are you refusing to answer my questions?

SARA: Listen, if you have a problem—

HISHAM: I don't have a problem. You have the problem.

SARA: Look, just—please just calm down.

HISHAM: I'm not upset. *(To audience.)* You people go home at night, you pat yourself on the back, you saw a play. Good. This woman makes some money. Good. You have no idea what it's like—

SARA: *(Overlap.)* Sir. Please. Please. If you would like to leave the theatre—

HISHAM: I do not want to leave.

SARA: Well, I'm sorry but—

HISHAM: I want to come into your house.

            Beat.

SARA: Excuse me?

HISHAM:	You are in your house, yes? It says here *(Opens program.),* "The action takes place inside Sara's house in Jaffa, Israel." Sara's house. I find that interesting. You are Canadian, yes?
SARA:	I just explained that…
HISHAM:	I have come to see the house. No offence. I'm sure the play is very good, but I came for the house.
SARA:	Maybe you don't understand. This is a piece of—
HISHAM:	I understand perfectly well. I am asking if I may be allowed to enter. Maybe you don't understand.
SARA:	No.
HISHAM:	I come from Ramallah
SARA:	Uh huh.
HISHAM:	Ramallah. In the West Bank.
SARA:	Yes, I know where Ramallah—
HISHAM:	I risked my life to get here. Do you understand what I'm saying? I risked my life.
SARA:	Sir, in another minute my stage manager—
HISHAM:	Listen to me—
SARA:	You need to know this—she is going to call the front of house, and they are going to call the police—
HISHAM:	No. NO.
SARA:	OK, just calm down.
HISHAM:	Tell her not to do that. I don't mean—I am not meaning—
SARA:	I am trying to give you a choice. If you would like to leave the theatre of your own accord—

HISHAM: I have nowhere to go, you understand? Please. My movements are severely restricted.

SARA: Yes, I understand.

HISHAM: You do?

SARA: Yes. And I sympathize, but I can't—

HISHAM: You what? —You sympathize?

SARA: Yes, I— Look. I understand. You're very upset. I think it's—it's awful, what's happening over there—

HISHAM: You do?

SARA: And I would really like to help but I…

HISHAM: You what.

SARA: I'm kind of busy.

            Beat.

HISHAM :   Yes. Of course. I'm sorry.

SARA: It's alright. If you could just—

HISHAM: *(To audience.)* I am deeply sorry for interrupting your evening's entertainment.

SARA: *(Motioning for him to go.)* Sir, if you could— Please.

            He starts to exit.

HISHAM: Is the lemon tree still there?

SARA: What.

HISHAM: In the backyard. Of your house. There was a lemon tree.

            Beat.

SARA: There's no tree.

HISHAM: What happened to it?

SARA: Nothing happened to it. What are you—

HISHAM: I'll bet you ten dollars there's a tree.

SARA: Look, I've worked on this play for a long time.

HISHAM: Congratulations.

SARA: So if you don't mind—

HISHAM: I just need to see the tree.

             Beat.

SARA: Sir. Through that door, there are plenty of trees. Perhaps you'll find the one you're looking for, if you just go through that door, and then out through the next one.

             Beat.

HISHAM: Perhaps.

SARA: If you need any help, the people at the box office—

HISHAM: No. Thank you.

             He exits.

SARA: I'm sorry. I think he'll…Everyone OK? I think he's gone, now. I'm just going to back up a bit. Uh.

             I can't remember what that point pertains to—seems appropriate—but I feel like I won the argument so I say to Marnie,

             "Can we get started, please?"

             Marnie goes to the window and looks out. "What do you believe in now, Sara?" She says. "Hey. I moved here didn't I?" *(To audience.)* I'm referring to my very recent move to Israel. No-one expected it, least of all me. Marnie picks up a letter that's sitting on one of the many unpacked boxes scattered around the room, it's from my...but she's distracted by something outside. "Too bad about that tree," she says. *(Beat. Confused.)* "What tree?" "If it weren't for the tree," she says, "you could put a tennis court in the backyard." *(Beat.)* Uh...I look out the window...and there's a lemon tree in my backyard. *(Pause.)* Um...sorry...there's an unexpected pause here while I try to remember the tree. Marnie puts her hand against my cheek and says, "You worry too much." Marnie never worries about anything. Marnie is beautiful because she is happy. She was even happy in high school. *(To Marnie.)* "How could anyone be happy in high school?" *(Beat.)* She smiles.

Of course, it's not true. I can remember Marnie looking worried. It's just kind of a touchy subject. "The first intifadah. *(Beat.)* You see? You see?" *(Beat.)* Marnie's not in the room anymore. She went to go put the cake in the fridge. *(Calling offstage.)* "I'm just going to go ahead then, OK? Feel free to jump in anytime." So. 1990. The height of the first intifadah, and Marnie and I decide we want to spend our summer in Israel. Every day on the news is another story about a Palestinian suicide bomber in Jerusalem, or the Israeli army shooting in the streets of Hebron. Same as today. But we were seventeen years old, "Weren't we, Marn?" And it's a good question, isn't it? What were we doing? What were we doing, going backpacking in a war zone?

Beat.

I'm wondering why I lit those candles.

Beat.

The crux of the story is that Marnie decided to go to Israel with a big tour group, instead of going backpacking with me. Three days before we leave for Israel, on the front page of the *Globe and Mail* is the story of an attempted PLO attack on a Tel Aviv beach. I remember it because it was the last day of school, and walking home that day, Marnie tells me she's not going at all. She says she's too scared to go, that her mom wants her to cancel the ticket. And I remember sitting on the curb with her and explaining very patiently that we absolutely had to go to Israel because the threat of terrorism was completely overblown by the mainstream media in an obvious attempt by massive corporate conglomerates to make billions of dollars off of the government's neo-fascist pursuit of war. Also, there were really hot guys in Israel, so.

Beat. Calls off stage.

"Marn? Where are you?" *(Beat.)* I'd rather not turn thirty in the dark by myself. It just doesn't seem like a very good omen. *(Beat.)* Marnie and I have an agreement. Every year, if we're not with someone, we usher in our birthdays together. The last five years, I wasn't able to, but now... Anyway, it's nice. It's, you know, comforting— It's tradition. Like these candles. My bubie lit the candles every Friday night. I do it maybe once a year and I feel like a hypocrite. Marnie would say I lit the candles as a desperate attempt to deny that Judaism has become meaningless to me. Or maybe she would say that I'm searching for something... I think. Uh. I think. *(Startled.)* "What?" "Aren't you going to answer that," Marnie says. "Answer what?" *(Sound of a doorbell.)* Uh. "The door," Marnie says. "There's no one at the door." *(Sound of an insistent doorbell.)* "Well, I don't know about in Israel, but in North America that would be a door," Marnie says. "Look, Marnie—there's no one at the door—"

HISHAM enters from backstage.

HISHAM: Hello? I am sorry to startle you. I rang the doorbell but nobody answered.

SARA: What are you—

HISHAM: Anyway, yes, pleased to meet you, *(Reaches for SARA's hand.)*, my name is Hisham Khatib, I am coming from Ramallah—

SARA: Listen—

HISHAM: *(Approaching Marnie.)* Hello, hello, I am Hisham, I am happy to make—

SARA: What are you— Who are you talking to?

HISHAM: I, well, I am introducing myself—

SARA: She's not in the room anymore.

HISHAM: Where did she—

SARA: Never mind. Now, what are you doing?

HISHAM: Do you mind if I …look around?.

SARA: Yes, actually. Sir, I would like to not have to call the police.

HISHAM: No. Please. I will be very quick. This is my first time, you know? I never— One of my uncles—he's in prison now—he came here once, maybe twenty years ago. But your grandmother, she was—she would not let him in.

SARA: I'm sorry?

HISHAM: Don't be. It's not your fault.

SARA: Listen—

HISHAM: You see, my family used to live in this house. For hundreds of years, they lived here. Until now, I have never even set foot in this house. But it is still mine.

SARA: This house?

HISHAM: Spiritually, you see, I have no other home. I have
               nowhere to go.

               (Beat.) My grandfather was born in this room—
               here, by the window. Can you believe it? Everyone
               gathered here for his birth, the brothers, the
               cousins. It's impossible but he says he
               remembers...being held. And of course he
               remembers the lemon tree—

SARA: I think you should leave.

HISHAM: All the men, they would sit here and drink coffee,
               and talk into the night... Do you see—over here—
               these lines? My grandfather told me about this,
               how his mother, my *(Arabic:* great-grandmother.)
               used to carve their heights into the wall.

SARA: No. My bubie did that. For my father.

HISHAM: I want to see the kitchen. He used to love to hide in
               the kitchen, when he was in trouble—

SARA: Alright. Enough.

HISHAM: Why? What's wrong?

SARA: I'm not— Just. Stop it.

HISHAM: I love this house.

SARA: Please get off the stage.

HISHAM: I love it, you see. Because they loved it. Like your
               Hebrew candles.

SARA: Hey. HEY. *(Removes candlesticks.)*

HISHAM: Because my ancestors cared for this house, I cannot
               just throw it away.

SARA: The program says "Sara's house".

HISHAM: That is not the point.

SARA: I think it is.

HISHAM: No. Please. I am trying to explain—

SARA: I need you to go. NOW.

             Beat.

HISHAM :   OK. I was leaving, earlier, as you suggested, but I heard you mention the intifadah, the PLO, terrorists.

SARA: I'm doing a play.

HISHAM: Ah. You are a writer.

SARA: An actor.

HISHAM: An actress.

SARA: An actor.

HISHAM: I realize now. You need help.

SARA: I'm sorry?

HISHAM: Why do you always say that?

SARA: Say what?

HISHAM: Nothing. You are performing a play about Palestinians, yes?

SARA: No.

HISHAM: No? You mentioned the intifadah, the PLO.

SARA: My play is not about Palestinians.

HISHAM: Of course it is.

SARA: Listen

HISHAM: Hisham.

SARA: Listen, Hisham, my play is not about politics.

HISHAM: Oh, I see.

SARA: My play is a personal story.

HISHAM: I see, a play about Palestinians is a political play, but a play about you, a Jew, is personal. Don't interrupt. It's very simple. You don't know anything about Palestinians. You've never heard our stories. I will help you. I will educate you about Palestinians and you will put this in your play.

                Beat.

SARA: So you saw the tree.

HISHAM: Yes.

SARA: So I guess you'll be heading home now.

HISHAM: You know, my grandfather, he is blind now, he is going to die soon.

SARA: Oh. I'm sorry.

HISHAM: Why? Is it your fault?

SARA: No, it's just…

HISHAM: He told me to come here and ask for a lemon from our tree.

SARA: My tree.

HISHAM: I come here for the lemon, I see that you are telling a story about our house, so I—

SARA: My house.

                Beat.

HISHAM: Are you alone? (*SARA looks out to the audience.*) No, I mean in life.

SARA: What kind of a question is that?

HISHAM: Well, no offence, Sara, but you seem like a very
           difficult woman. Very argumentative.

SARA: Uh huh.

HISHAM: And you seem to need to possess things. It's that
           security issue, isn't it? I'm not trying to upset you,
           I can see you are a little upset, but I'm just saying
           your husband must have a very hard time. Maybe
           he calls you controlling, unfeminine, I don't know.

SARA: I don't have a husband. And there's no need to get
           personal.

HISHAM: I thought your play was personal. *(SARA sits on the
           edge of the stage.)*

           What are you doing? Sara. *(Beat.)* Sara. *(Beat.)* Are
           you ignoring me now? *(Arabic:* Fine.) *(Pause.)* Look,
           I'm sorry if I hurt your feelings, I didn't...I
           wouldn't want to...do that. Sometimes I—what? I
           put my leg in my mouth. *(Beat.)* Why are you
           laughing?

SARA: I'm not laughing, I'm smiling.

HISHAM: You are...? *(Arabic:* My God, this woman will drive
           me crazy. Grandfather give me patience...etc.)*

SARA: Hey. HEY. Calm down.

HISHAM: Why? I'm not upset. Are you upset? Typically
           Western to confuse passion for emotion. You have
           a conversation like a tennis match. Very polite.
           Very quiet. Back and forth, back and forth.

SARA: What's wrong with that? At least it's, you know

HISHAM: Civilized?

           Beat.

SARA: Look. If I give you the lemon will you go away and promise not to come back?

HISHAM: No. Why would I do that? This was my grandfather's house and one day, inshallah, it will be in my family again.

SARA: This was my bubie's home.

HISHAM: No.

SARA: She was here in 1948. She was in the Holocaust. She lost both her parents, they were shot in the streets. She came here because she had nowhere else to go. No country would take her.

HISHAM: Yes, but whose country was it before she came? Think, Sara. My family lived here for eight hundred years.

SARA: Well, whose country was it before that?

HISHAM: Oh please.

SARA: What? Why stop at eight hundred? Two thousand years ago the Romans were here. Five thousand years ago, guess what? The Jews lived here, until they were thrown out. How far back should we go?

HISHAM: Sara—

SARA: No, really, should we talk biblically? God promised the land of Israel to the Jewish people. Look it up. Genesis, chapter 13, verse 14. HAH, HAH. *(Beat.)* I was Bible Contest Champion at my synagogue three years in a row.

                Beat.

HISHAM: You are a lonely woman, yes?

SARA: No.

HISHAM: Ah.

Beat.

SARA: Listen—

HISHAM: I'm surprised at you, Sara.

SARA: You...what...you don't even know me.

HISHAM: I thought you lit the candles because you felt something...inexplicable. A passion. The same reason I came to this house. The same reason my grandfather wants that lemon so much, he wakes up crying for it every morning. A different lemon, a different house, it will not work. But now I know, that's not why you light those candles.

SARA: Listen—

HISHAM: It's your security blanket, isn't it? Lighting the candles, Yom Kippur, Israel, this play. You don't believe in any of it, except to hang on to it. The only motivation is fear.

SARA: That's not true.

HISHAM: Oh, you're right. Forgive me. We can't forget guilt. The worst kind of liberal guilt that results in tokenism on all sides. This is your token play, that is your token Jewish tradition, I am your token Arab—

SARA: Hey. Nobody's forcing you to stay.

HISHAM: God forbid you should actually believe in something.

SARA: I...

HISHAM: Let it go.

SARA: I can't.

HISHAM: YOU WON'T.

Beat.

SARA: I offered you a seat. If you want to go, go.

HISHAM: Oh no. I am not giving you that satisfaction. To say you invited me to stay but I refused. It will be 1948 all over again.

SARA: What?

HISHAM: I can see the headlines: "Civilized Jew Invites Uncivilized Palestinian to Stay. He Refuses. War for Sixty Years."

SARA: OK.

HISHAM: "Everyone Agrees He Deserves What He Gets."

SARA: OK. Alright. Point taken.

HISHAM: Anyway, I would like to see this story that has nothing to do with me.

SARA: Suit yourself.

HISHAM: I will sit over here.

SARA: Fine.

HISHAM: The ball's in your court.

SARA: What?

HISHAM: I won't say another word.

SARA: I would appreciate that.

> *SARA motions to the Stage Manager. The lights dim. Beat.*

HISHAM: Go ahead.

> *Beat.*

SARA: I think. Uh. I think. *(Startled. To Marnie.)* "What? I wasn't talking about anything. I was stalling, actually. I was talking about...tennis."

Marnie and I used to play tennis almost every day. In my old room, hanging on the wall over my bed, was a photo of the great Billie Jean King in mid-smash and, underneath it, her quote about tennis: "A perfect combination of violent action taking place in an atmosphere of total tranquility." The photo was given to me by my grandfather, my zaydie, for my thirteenth birthday. My zaydie said that when he turned thirteen, during the Depression, his mother sold her fur coat in Kensington Market to get him a tennis racquet. But when he went to a local club to play, there was a sign on the door—they still had these signs in Toronto: "No Jews, Blacks, or Dogs." And he was so mad. He just wanted to find someone to fight.

"What?" *(Beat.)* Marnie says that's why he married my bubie. "Thanks, Marn. Thanks for your help." She laughs—Marnie has the best laugh—and for some reason I feel a sudden pang that I'm not in synagogue with my family for Yom Kippur services. My father will be singing in the choir. My mother will have saved a seat for me despite the fact that I'm not even in the country. I haven't been to shul in thirteen years.

(To Marnie.) "Oh, god, Rabbi Bergman called me before I left and asked me to meet with him. I thought he was going to make me apologize three times for not coming to shul—"

The phone rings.

What…

The phone rings.

Um…

HISHAM: Go ahead.

SARA: What?

HISHAM: Answer the phone.

SARA: Hello?

               HISHAM plays Rabbi Bergman.

RABBI: We've got a bit of a situation, here.

SARA: Rabbi?

RABBI: How are ya, Sara.

SARA: Oh, I'm not feeling so well.

RABBI: I hear your birthday's coming up. The big 3-0.

SARA: That's right.

RABBI: Tick tock. Tick tock.

SARA: What kind of a situation, Rabbi?

RABBI: Well, it's tradition, you know, to ask a member of the congregation to give a dvar torah on Yom Kippur.

SARA: I'm sorry, a what?

RABBI: A dvar t—a sermon, Sara, a sermon.

SARA: Oh right.

RABBI: Anyway, you can pick the subject, as long as you connect it to Genesis, Chapter one, Verse one, OK?

SARA: OK what?

RABBI :   OK you'll do the sermon at the Mincha, the afternoon service, next week.

SARA: Me? Why me?

RABBI: Why you? Come on. Who won all those bible contests in grade five? Who was the President of the Temple Youth Group? You were a star, Sara, a star. We want you to shine, that's all.

SARA: Someone cancelled, huh?

RABBI: That lousy Morty Bernstein, always backing out at
           the last minute.

SARA: Look, I can't

RABBI: Come on, Sara. Please. This isn't just any Yom
           Kippur, you know. With everything going on in
           the Middle East, everybody's frightened, they're
           looking for answers.

SARA: I don't have answers—

RABBI: You were very outspoken in the youth group. I
           remember. Always going on about peace.

SARA: I was seventeen.

RABBI: I'm saying you can do your sermon on peace.
           Wouldn't that be great? Just don't get too political,
           we have enough problems. And talk about
           Genesis, Chapter one, Verse one.

SARA: Rabbi, I haven't been to shul in thirteen years.

RABBI: So? We haven't moved if that's what you're
           worried about.

SARA: I don't even know if I believe in God.

RABBI: So.

SARA: So?

RABBI: Neither do I.

SARA: What?

RABBI: Every time I pray it's a struggle.

SARA: Wait a minute.

RABBI: It's called faith, poopie.

SARA: Uh huh.

RABBI: In Judaism, you speak first, ask questions later.

SARA: Well some people would call that hypocrisy, Rabbi. Some people would call that obeying orders, or falling into line, or leaving one's capacity for independent thought at the door.

RABBI: Uh huh. So will you do it?

SARA: Rabbi. You want me to stand up in front of a thousand people and act like I believe something that I don't on one of the holiest days of the year?

RABBI: OK.

SARA: Rabbi.

RABBI: Faith is not an answer. It's a struggle. Just like life.

SARA: Uh huh.

RABBI: Sometimes you have to enter the fight.

            Beat.

SARA: I don't think so.

RABBI: What do you believe, Sara?

SARA: As much as I appreciate the invitation—

RABBI: WHAT DO YOU BELIEVE?

SARA: At this time, I really don't have anything to say.

            Silence.

SARA: Huh.

HISHAM: What does that mean?

SARA: Nothing. Just. Huh.

HISHAM: Did you…I mean, was I—

SARA: Shhh.

HISHAM:	What's wrong.
SARA:	SHHHH. Stop talking. Shit. I can't remember my next line.
HISHAM:	Can I help?
SARA:	No.

She makes a noise of frustration.

HISHAM:	What? What is it?
SARA:	Everything's messed up now. I can't...I don't even know what comes next.
HISHAM:	It's OK.
SARA:	No, it's not OK. Nothing is OK. I don't know what you think, but I find theatre quite difficult you know. It's lonely. And people cough. They cough and you don't know if it's because they're bored or because they're sick and in the winter it gets really confusing.
HISHAM:	Calm down.
SARA:	Calm down? Calm down? This is THEATRE. No one's calm in theatre. Except for them. They're so fucking calm they could be sleeping.
HISHAM:	Sara.
SARA:	*(Hyperventilates.)* Sometimes it gets so quiet that I think maybe I'm completely alone. Like in the universe. Maybe I don't even exist. Maybe you don't either.
HISHAM:	Of course I do.
SARA:	Oh typically Palestinian to think you exist. Oh god. I need air.
HISHAM:	What are you doing?

SARA: There's no air *(Hyperventilates.)*. I can't handle this. I don't like *(hyperventilates.)*. I'm not good with *(Hyperventilates.)*.

HISHAM: What?

SARA: I'm having a *(Hyperventilates.)*, a *(Hyperventilates.)*.

HISHAM: A WHAT?

SARA: A PANIC ATTACK.

> *HISHAM slaps SARA. SARA slaps HISHAM harder. Pause. SARA gets into child's pose.*

HISHAM: What are you doing?

SARA: Shhh.

HISHAM: Sara.

SARA: I'm in child's pose.

HISHAM: It looks like you are doing the Salaah.

SARA: I don't pray.

HISHAM: Neither do I. It just looked—

SARA: But for some reason this posture just makes me feel safe, you know?

HISHAM: Yes.

SARA: The world is a crazy place and sometimes you just need a little…

HISHAM: Peace?

SARA: Security.

HISHAM: Of course.

> *Pause. SARA breathes.*

SARA: What are you doing?

HISHAM:	I'm sitting down.
SARA:	Why? Why are you sitting down? In my play.
HISHAM:	Don't get excited—
SARA:	What are you doing?
HISHAM:	I'm...standing...
SARA:	No. In the larger sense. To my play. You're ruining my play.
HISHAM:	I thought I was helping.
SARA:	They're all going to think I'm boring now.
HISHAM:	What?
SARA:	They're going to think I'm boring. On my own.
HISHAM:	Sara. Listen to me. They love you.
SARA:	No.
HISHAM:	Yes. You are very interesting to watch.
SARA:	No, I'm not.
HISHAM:	Yes, you are.
SARA:	I feel fat.
HISHAM:	Don't be ridiculous. You are very attractive.
SARA:	Oh OK.
HISHAM:	Sara. I'm getting angry now. You are an exciting woman. A little crazy, it's true, but so are all women. You just need a strong man.
SARA:	Oh god.
HISHAM:	Oh. She's getting offended. I'm sorry, you must need a weak man.
SARA:	Maybe I don't need any man.

HISHAM:	That's what I like about you. You exude something…independent.
SARA:	Are you flirting with me?
HISHAM:	No. Unless. Do you want me to?

Beat.

SARA:	Hah.
HISHAM:	Hah?
SARA:	You said I was argumentative.
HISHAM:	I know.
SARA:	And lonely. And insecure.
HISHAM:	You're also fiery, independent and vulnerable. And you know what else?
SARA:	Controlling, maybe? Unfeminine?
HISHAM:	You have beautiful lips.

Beat.

SARA:	What do you want?
HISHAM:	What?
SARA:	You're up to something. What is it?
HISHAM:	I thought it was fairly obvious.
SARA:	I'm not an idiot, Hisham. What do you want?
HISHAM:	What did you think of my performance?
SARA:	You want a compliment?
HISHAM:	Some feedback would be nice. I am human, after all. I have my own insecurities.

Beat.

SARA:	It wasn't bad.
HISHAM:	Thank you.
SARA:	I wasn't sure about the one moment—
HISHAM:	The one where I did the—
SARA:	Exactly.
HISHAM:	Too obvious.
SARA:	Possibly.
HISHAM:	Too on the nose.
SARA:	Well.
HISHAM:	No offence.

Beat.

SARA:	What do you mean, 'no offence'.

Beat.

HISHAM:	Nothing.
SARA:	You're not referring to my—
HISHAM:	No, no—oh, no, not THAT, I didn't mean—
SARA:	No, I didn't think you would, of course not. Sorry.
HISHAM:	Sorry.
SARA:	Sorry.

Awkward moment. They laugh. SARA notices the audience.

Oh. Sorry. Um. We'll be with you in just a moment. *(Beat. Moves off to the side, motions for HISHAM to follow.)* So what now?

HISHAM:	Now?

SARA: Well, I'm a little lost. I guess I just keep going, right?

HISHAM: You don't have to.

SARA: Oh god. It was boring, wasn't it?

HISHAM: No. Sara. I just…I think you and I make a very good team.

               Beat.

SARA: I don't even like one-woman shows. *(Beat.)* I mean, of course. I don't mean that. That's not what I mean. Of course I like one-woman shows. I find them more interesting when they include other actors, that's all.

HISHAM: Yes.

SARA: It's more diverse.

               Beat.

HISHAM: Are you suggesting…?

SARA: No. I don't know. Maybe. What do you think?

HISHAM: Well, I could try…

SARA: *(Indicating audience.)* Should we ask them? For their opinion.

HISHAM: God, no. I mean, they're nice and they look…clean but why should we give up our…our…

SARA: Our power. Our control.

HISHAM: Our rights. Our rights. Art is not a democracy. This is our show.

SARA: My show.

HISHAM: Of course. We are the masters of our fate.

SARA: My fate. *(Catches herself.)* Sorry. So what should we do?

HISHAM: I think we should do it.

SARA: You do?

            HISHAM holds out his hand. They shake hands,
            very excited.

HISHAM: I think this calls for something.

SARA: Like, what, a drink?

HISHAM: No. Something official. For the program.

SARA: The what.

HISHAM: To put in the program.

SARA: Wait. What does the program say?

HISHAM: It only has your information.

SARA: No. What does the program say comes next?

            Suddenly, program inserts drop like propaganda
            leaflets from above the audience. They contain
            HISHAM's information and a slightly new play
            title.

HISHAM: *(Gets one from the audience.)* It says, 'Territories: A
            Dialogue'.

SARA: A dialogue? What does that mean?

HISHAM: Discussion. Chat. Discourse.

SARA: I don't know about this. I don't really like change.
            Look at your bio!

HISHAM: Shhh. I'm having an idea. Why don't we start by
            introducing each other? The audience hasn't
            officially met me. These pamphlets are a good first
            step, but—

SARA: But—but what? They gave you equal billing. What
            else do you want?

HISHAM: Sara. By introducing each other, we are announcing a new partnership. Remember? We are a team.

SARA: OK, OK, so I will introduce you—hold on a sec— (*She gets a pencil and an insert and starts writing.*)

HISHAM: And I will introduce you.

SARA: You don't need to introduce me. I've been here since the beginning.

HISHAM: So have I.

           Beat.

SARA: And then we'll have a 'dialogue', right?

HISHAM: Exactly.

SARA: As a way of introducing you to the audience.

HISHAM: As a way of introducing us both to the audience.

SARA: Hisham.

HISHAM: Yes.

SARA: I'm getting annoyed.

HISHAM: Of course. Let's begin. Music!

           Music. This next bit is upbeat, cheery and quick, a la 'Entertainment Tonight'.

SARA: Ladies and Gentlemen, we have as our guest today a Palestinian human rights worker and journalist.

HISHAM: Ah-lan wa-salaam. Here with us today is a North American Jewish woman who works as a writer, performer, and peace activist.

SARA: In 1948, his family was forcibly removed from their home in Jaffa, where they had lived for 800 years, and placed in a refugee camp.

HISHAM: She grew up in Canada, where she and her family considered themselves, inexplicably, both liberals and Zionists at the same time.

            Beat.

SARA: Hisham now lives in Ramallah, in the West Bank. He considers himself a secular Muslim, if there is such a thing.

HISHAM: Sara was raised a Reform Jew, which means that she will go to synagogue once a year on High Holidays, will order bacon but not "pork", and will date non-Jewish men in order to scare her mother, but will ultimately marry a Jew.

SARA: Hisham enjoys the company of non-Muslim women when travelling outside of the Occupied Territories, but ultimately is looking for an independent-minded secular Palestinian woman who looks good in a scarf. Please welcome as my guest, Hisham Khatib.

HISHAM: Please welcome as my guest, Sara Levine.

            Beat.

SARA: And now for your Morning Smile: A priest, a rabbi, and an imam walk into a bar. The bartender says, "Is this a joke?" *(She laughs. HISHAM doesn't.)* Alright. I believe I have the first question.

HISHAM: Of course you do.

            Beat.

SARA: What does that mean.

HISHAM: You wrote the script so clearly everything is slanted in your favour.

SARA: I don't think…

HISHAM: No, please. I do not want to look ungrateful. I do

	not want the late night news to report, "Palestinian Man Ungrateful For The Crumbs He Was Offered." Go ahead.

SARA: Okey dokey. *(Reading.)* "Hisham, do you, as a Palestinian, find it difficult to condemn terrorist groups like Hamas who use violence as a means of achieving their political aims?"

            Beat.

HISHAM: That's the first question?

SARA: Yup.

HISHAM: I would say that I oppose violence, yes.

SARA: So you are against Hamas.

HISHAM: Hamas is a complex organization, it is not only a militant group, it also serves the needs of the community—

SARA: By blowing people up?

HISHAM: The use of violence to achieve freedom is regrettable—

SARA: Regrettable?

HISHAM: But it is certainly not unheard of. Your own people used terrorism in the struggle for the State of Israel—

SARA: So you are in favour of the use of violence.

HISHAM: I am merely saying that we did not invent it. Or are you forgetting about the Irgun bombing of the King David Hotel in 1946, which killed 91 people— 28 Britons, 41 Arabs, 17 Jews and 5 others—

SARA: *(Overlap.)* It's a simple question, Hisham. Do you or do you not oppose the use of violence to achieve a Palestinian state?

HISHAM: I will oppose my people's violence if you will oppose your people's violence.

SARA: My people's violence is a response to your people's violence.

HISHAM :   I would say the same.

             Beat.

SARA: How exciting. It's only the beginning of the dialogue and already we're finding common ground. Let's keep the ball rolling. Your question, Hisham.

             She passes HISHAM his question. HISHAM looks at it.

HISHAM: I do not like my question.

SARA: Why? What's wrong with it?

HISHAM: It says: "Do you believe in a two-state solution?"

SARA: And the answer is, I absolutely believe that the Palestinians deserve their own state beside Israel, and that it should consist of the West Bank and Gaza.

HISHAM: How kind of you.

SARA: Thank you.

HISHAM: No, really, very generous.

SARA: Thank you very much.

HISHAM: Just imagine, for a moment, really, just close your eyes for a moment and imagine if somebody came into your house, just walked into your house, and pushed you and your family into the bathroom.

SARA: OK.

HISHAM: And then the discussion became—not could you

have your house back, or even part of your house—but whether or not you and your entire family were entitled to live in the bathroom.

SARA: Do you mind if I build on your metaphor?

HISHAM: Go right ahead.

SARA: OK, A, it was our house too, before it was your house, and we were kicked out of it, and certainly not offered the bathroom. B, we invited you to stay in the house and you not only refused, you called all your Arab buddies to come and try to push us into the backyard pool, and C, we can't let you out of the bathroom because there is no doubt in anyone's mind what you'd do to us if you got out.

HISHAM: You're not hearing me. The point is, the question frames the discussion that follows, right? And the question itself, the question of a two-state solution, is biased. It narrows the possible options. It seems like a fair question, but it isn't.

SARA: I'm willing to be fair.

HISHAM: OK. I would like to discuss the possibility that I rewrite this entire script.

            Beat.

SARA: It's not going to happen.

HISHAM: Why not?

SARA: Because.

HISHAM: Because?

SARA: Why? What would you want to do with it?

HISHAM: Don't you trust me?

SARA: Typically Palestinian, to want to have a discussion about the discussion. No wonder you never get anywhere.

HISHAM: Typically Western, to compose the whole script before sitting down, and then pretend that everything is improvised.

SARA: Typically Arab to enter into an agreement without any intention of following through.

HISHAM: Typically Jewish to… *(Catches himself. Beat.)* What if we share it?

SARA: What.

HISHAM: The script.

SARA: What, like you write the parts about you, and I write the parts about me?

HISHAM: That's one way of doing it.

SARA: How do we decide who gets how many parts?

HISHAM: Or we could write it together.

            Silence.

            Sara?

            Silence.

            Sara?

            Silence.

SARA: I can't—

HISHAM: We can make this work—

SARA: I can't. I'm sorry. I, uh, I made a mistake.

HISHAM: You offered me a partnership. I want to be an equal.

SARA: This is. It's way too fast.

HISHAM: I have rights, Sara. Would you like to hear about my rights?

SARA: No.

HISHAM: Let's talk about 1948.

SARA: Oh god no.

HISHAM: *(Stands and announces.)* The 1948 United Nations Universal Declaration of Human Rights. The 1966 International Covenant on Civil and Political Rights.

SARA: Stop it, Hisham.

HISHAM: Oh, yes, I forgot. Those don't apply to Palestinians. How about the Hague Convention of 1907 and the Geneva Conventions—

SARA: I SAID STOP IT.

HISHAM: So you are breaking off the partnership.

SARA: Sorry.

HISHAM: Sorry. This is an apology. Say it three times. If I don't forgive you, God will.

SARA: We're just. Very different, Hisham.

HISHAM: Yes. You have everything and I have nothing.

SARA: So I should give up my play.

HISHAM: You should share. Fairly.

SARA: The last person who told me to share fairly was my ex-husband and he took half my stuff.

            Beat.

HISHAM: Your ex-husband.

SARA: Yes.

            Beat.

HISHAM: What was his name?

SARA: Alan. *(Beat.)* Why are you laughing?

HISHAM: I'm not laughing, I'm smiling. I can't picture you married. And I certainly can't picture you married to someone named Alan.

SARA: Yeah. Well. Blink and you'd miss it.

HISHAM: Divorce has made you bitter.

SARA: No, marriage made me bitter. My ex-husband made me bitter. Typically Palestinian to blame the solution and not the problem.

HISHAM: Typically Western to think separation is a solution.

SARA: I didn't just...You don't know...

HISHAM: Let me ask you, Sara, on a daily basis what makes you more upset—the fact that your people are oppressing another people, taking their land, demolishing their homes, building a Security Wall that is, in essence, forcing them into ghettos—

SARA: Or?

HISHAM: Or the fact that your husband left you and took half your stuff?

           Beat.

SARA: I don't like the question.

HISHAM: I am sorry for your personal suffering, Sara, but it doesn't change the fact that you are privileged.

SARA: Oh, I see.

HISHAM: You have power now. Your personal story is— Forgive me, but it is irrelevant.

SARA: Irrelevant? What about your grandfather and your lemon tree—

HISHAM: These are simply examples of a larger suffering. The fact that it is personal to me is not important.

SARA: Oh, I think it's very important. I think this whole thing is personal. I think you came here today to punish me for some personal reason and—hey— I'd like to hear it.

HISHAM: There is nothing to tell.

SARA: I thought you wanted to be in showbiz.

HISHAM: I am inspired by my people's land. By their rights to that land. By their *rights*, which your people have consistently ignored and violated—

SARA: Well, I hate to tell you, Hisham, but theatre's about stories. Not propaganda, not rhetoric— I tell you what. I'll give you an audition. *(Walks into the audience.)* Should have done that before, actually. That's the way we usually get jobs in theatre. We don't usually just show up in the middle of a play and—you know—talk. Not in North America anyway. It's part of that civilized thing. So anyway I'll sit out here—way back here—and that way you've got the stage all to yourself. OK? Hisham Khatib, tell us your personal story.

             Pause. HISHAM is unable to speak. Slowly, a medley of sound and projected images of HISHAM's life in the West Bank grows into a cacophony and then suddenly ceases.

SARA: Anytime, Hisham.

             Silence.

SARA: *(Sort of 'sotto voce'.)* Typical.

HISHAM: What did you say?

SARA: I said typically Palestinian to waste an opportunity.

> *Beat. SARA approaches the stage.*

HISHAM: I would like to try again.

SARA: Really.

HISHAM: Yes.

SARA: You're ready for your close-up now.

HISHAM: That's right, I am ready now. So please get off the stage.

SARA: Perhaps you'd like to apologize first for being so disruptive.

HISHAM: I have every right to share this stage

SARA: Are you alone?

HISHAM: What?

SARA: I mean in life. You're a very demanding person, Hisham. Your wife must have a very hard time.

HISHAM: My wife…I don't have a wife.

SARA: Really.

HISHAM: I am glad you are finding the humour. Since you started with a joke, is it permissible to end with a quotation?

SARA: Is it funny?

HISHAM: "Do not press a desperate foe too hard."

> *Beat.*

SARA: I don't get it.

HISHAM: You are an intelligent woman. I'm sure you will figure it out.

> *HISHAM exits. Beat.*

SARA: "Marnie? Oh, thank god, I thought you'd left. No,
             honey, everything's fine, everything's just...fine.

             Beat.

             What?

             Oh, let's see, uh, you had a nap, and I...I watched
             the news. Oh, you know, same old, same old.
             People dying in Africa, war in the Middle East, not
             one good joke the entire program. What?— No,
             you can't have the cake yet, Marnie, we're fasting.
             Because we're guilty of something, that's why. I
             don't know what but we're just supposed to keep
             apologizing for another...twenty hours." Ten
             minutes to my thirtieth birthday and twenty hours
             to God closing the Book of Life for another year.
             God writes in the Book of Life the names of those
             who will live and those who will die, and the
             decision is based, at least partly, on repentance. It's
             the ultimate reality show. Jewish Survivor.
             Whoever feels the guiltiest wins.

             Pause.

             I'm ready to apologize now.

             *HISHAM emerges from the shadows/stands up in
             the audience. Very long pause.*

             I apologize to myself. *(Beat.)* For my fashion
             choices in the 1980's.

             HISHAM retreats.

             And for sleeping with men that I should not have
             slept with. And for not sleeping with men that I
             should not have slept with. And for marrying a
             man that I should not have slept with. And for
             being alone. Yeah, that, and for not doing things
             that I wanted to do at a time when I really should
             have done them. Amen.

Beat.

I wanted to move to Israel when I was younger. I wanted to make aliya. "I never told you that." I went to Israel when I was seventeen years old with this romantic idea of joining in The Great Zionist Struggle. Marnie went to Israel to meet boys. I ended up getting drunk and fooling around with the first non-Jewish boy I met. Mark Gillespie. He was busking in Dizengoff Square in Tel Aviv, a beautiful British boy playing Beatles songs. "You were there with your tour group, Marn, you remember. We saw each other in the square..." And then I saw Mark.

I forgot all about Marnie. I pushed my way through the crowd of girls, marched right up to him and said— *(She turns and HISHAM is there.)* Uh, I said...

MARK: *(In Manchester accent.)* You got a request?

SARA: *(Becomes seventeen-year-old SARA.)* 'Happiness is a Warm Gun.' *(To the audience.)* The White Album.

MARK: Do you want to go for a drink?

SARA: Like, I don't know, OK. *(To Marnie, back in present.)* "What? Of course I said goodbye to you. If I didn't say goodbye to you, then how did we make a plan to meet in Jerusalem the following Friday night? *(Beat.)* Thank you." *(To Mark.)* So, um, Mark, did you know that Pink Floyd is going to play 'The Wall' at the Berlin Wall? It's so symbolic.

MARK :   Come a little closer.

SARA: OK. *(To Marnie.)* "What? No. No, I won't apologize. Because we're not at that part of the story yet and anyway I don't agree with you."

Pause. To audience.

Marnie's not in the room anymore.

MARK: Helloooo…

SARA: *(As seventeen-year-old SARA.)* Sorry. My friend, she's, like, mad at me.

MARK: Bollocks.

           He grabs her and they start to dance. It gets very sexy. Suddenly SARA pulls away.

SARA: Mark, can I trust you?

MARK: You can only trust people you know, sweetie, and we just met.

SARA: *(To audience.)* He's so honest.

           They dance. It gets more sexy.

SARA: I should, um, I should go.

MARK: Go? You just got here.

SARA: Yeah, but I should

MARK: Should what?

SARA: I don't even know you.

MARK: What's there to know?

SARA: Do you believe in God?

MARK: What?

SARA: I'm just, I'm trying to decide what to do with my life—

MARK: You're a real trip.

SARA: and whether or not I should move here and be more spiritual and I'm feeling really guilty about my friend.

MARK: Sweetheart. God is Everywhere. He is here. And there. And there.

SARA: Oh.

MARK: So should we *do it*?

SARA: What?

MARK: You know. Should we *do it*?

            Beat.

SARA: *(To audience.)* I said no to Mark. I made a promise. I made a promise to Marnie that I wouldn't lose my virginity unless she was there.

HISHAM: Should we do it?

SARA: But I never thought about God the same way again.

HISHAM: Sara.

SARA: I would like to believe in something.

HISHAM: I am asking you.

SARA: I said no.

HISHAM: There is a relationship here, Sara. Whether you like it or not.

SARA: You know what I think?

HISHAM: There is a very small window of opportunity here—

SARA: You don't want me to finish my story.

HISHAM: —to do this willingly, in a friendly way.

SARA: Are you threatening me?

HISHAM: I am telling you I am desperate and you must listen to me—

SARA:	"Marnie!"
HISHAM:	I won't let you write me out of this play.
SARA:	"Where the hell have you been?" She puts her feet up on my coffee-table again, and doesn't answer for a while. "What's wrong? Apologize for what?"
HISHAM:	Sara! Look at me!
SARA:	Marnie wants me to apologize for the fact that— "I want you to know that I kept that plan. I went to Jerusalem to meet you."
HISHAM:	WHAT ARE YOU DOING?
SARA:	"I can prove it. I went to the Western Wall."

HISHAM plays Man.

MAN:	I SAID WHAT ARE YOU DOING?
SARA:	"And after I had dinner with this rabbi, Rabbi Gopnik."
MAN:	ANSWER ME.
SARA:	Just let me finish. "I went onto the rooftop. And I wrote a prayer for you, for both of us, for our future—"
MAN:	OR I WILL CALL SECURITY.

Beat. SARA plays her seventeen-year-old self.

SARA:	No. No. I'm just. I'm just looking.
MAN:	You're American.
SARA:	Canadian.
MAN:	Whatever. It's very dangerous up here. You could be shot.
SARA:	Shot? I was just trying to—

MAN: This isn't Canada, you know. You're in Jerusalem now. You can't just walk around on rooftops. They could mistake you for a sniper. Come down.

SARA: No.

Beat.

MAN: No?

SARA: No...thank you?

MAN: How old are you?

SARA: Seventeen.

MAN: Seventeen.

SARA: So?

MAN: Life is simple, huh?

SARA: Not really.

MAN: Tell me—what's your name?

SARA: Sara.

MAN: Tell me, Sara, you want to make aliyah? Huh? You want to move to Israel?

SARA: I don't know.

MAN: You don't know? Then what are you doing here?

SARA: I just, like I ate dinner with Rabbi Gopnik. In his apartment, downstairs

MAN: Rabbi Gopnik.

SARA: Yes.

MAN: Rabbi Gopnik.

SARA: Yes. Do you know him?

MAN: Oh I know, I know Gopnik. Believe me, I'm no
              stranger to Rabbi Gopnik. First of all, my
              apartment's right below his. He's meshugah. Picks
              up forty people every Friday night at the Wall,
              feeds them out of his own pocket.

SARA: I think it's nice.

MAN: Nice? Ya, you would, what do you know. Nice.
              You know what's nice? Canadians are nice.
              Canadians would not take a bunch of strangers,
              who knows who, bring them home, and get them
              to sing and dance all over the neighbour's ceiling.
              That's not nice.

SARA: OK, stop yelling.

MAN: (Yelling.) Who's yelling? What, Canadians have to
              whisper?

SARA: I think, I think he just wants to, you know, inspire
              people.

MAN: Jews.

SARA: Well, of course, Jews.

MAN: What of course? What, we Israelis are supposed to
              inspire all the Jews now? Let me tell you, I went to
              New York City, nobody even picked me up at the
              airport.

SARA: What does that have to do—

MAN: Life is not simple, Sara. You come here, you have
              an expectation, we're all waiting with open arms
              for you. To inspire you. Then you go home to
              Canada. You sleep safe in your bed. Good. Rabbi
              Gopnik pats himself on the back. Good. You've got
              no idea what it's like here.

SARA: I know about the Palestinians, I know about the
              intifadah—

MAN: Oh really? Did you happen to notice the Arabs singing their Friday night prayers at the Dome of the Rock?

SARA: No.

MAN: No, you wouldn't have. Because every time the Arabs sing their prayers, Rabbi Gopnik starts singing to drown them out. No matter where he is in the service. I've seen him do it in the middle of a conversation, suddenly start singing at the top of his lungs. Now that's denial.

SARA: Maybe he just likes to sing.

MAN: Sara, Sara, Sara. I'm trying to tell you, it's complicated. Here you fart and someone starts a holy war. Come here. Since we're up here risking our lives, you might as well learn something. We're in the Old City, right? Very famous. How big do you think it is? I'll tell you. The whole thing takes up less than a square kilometre. Right there's the Kotel, or the Western Wall or the Wailing Wall, whatever you want to call it, OK? The last remaining wall of the Second Temple, destroyed in 70 C.E. by the Roman army. Now look up. Not all the way up. Just. There. That's the Temple Mount, where God instructed Abraham to sacrifice his son, Isaac, right? You've heard of Abraham, right?

SARA: Yeah.

MAN: Well, I've got news for you. The Temple Mount is also known as Haram-ash Sharif, where Mohammed supposedly leapt up to heaven. Is that a coincidence or what? And right over there, just a few hundred meters east, right where we Jews believe the messiah will come strolling back to us and bring us two thousand years of peace, is the Mount of Olives, where Jesus also apparently ascended to heaven. Why would God do that? The three major monotheistic religions—coulda been anywhere in the world—all within a square kilometre. Why?

SARA: I don't know.

MAN: I don't know either. Maybe we're supposed to get to know each other. Have a block party. Lend each other power tools, drive each other's kids to school, be good neighbours. I don't know.

SARA: Well, I—

MAN: Maybe God intended us to have a relationship. He's very sneaky, God. He squishes us together, on this tiny strip of land. "Deal with it," He says. Like a marriage, for better or for worse.

            Beat.

SARA: I have to go now.

MAN: Oh now you have to go? I tell you to leave, you want to stay, I tell you to stay, you have to go. Just like a woman.

SARA: For your information, I came up here to do something, but you started talking and now I have to go. My friend Marnie is supposed to meet me on Ben Yehuda Street in, like, half an hour.

MAN: Ben Yehuda Street. Another dangerous place.

SARA: Goodbye. It was nice meeting you.

MAN: OK, OK, hold your horses. Marnie will wait five minutes, if she's such a friend. *(Beat.)* So, what did you come up here for?

SARA: To write a prayer. Rabbi Gopnik told us to, he said he would put all our prayers into the cracks in the Wall tomorrow.

MAN: Oh, he did, huh?

SARA: I just…I couldn't think with all those people around. Anyway, it doesn't matter, it's too late, now.

MAN: I tell you what. You write the prayer, I'll handle it for you.

SARA: Really?

MAN: Really.

SARA: Because I promised my parents I would do this. They were worried, you know, that if I backpacked through Israel by myself that I wouldn't do anything serious, you know, that I would just go drinking and go to nightclubs, and even though, OK, I have done a bit of that, I think that they could trust me to go to the Wailing Wall. I'm not an idiot.

Beat.

MAN: Write your prayer, Sara.

Beat. She writes.

Tell me Sara, what do you believe?

SARA: What?

MAN: At home, do you pray?

SARA: Not really.

MAN: So why do you want to pray now?

SARA: I don't know. I'm here.

MAN: Here.

SARA: At the Wall. Rabbi Bergman—that's my rabbi back home—he says that the Wall is like a direct phone line to God.

She gives the prayer to him.

MAN: I'll bet He has a great long-distance plan. *(Beat.)* It's a joke.

SARA: There's a story, I don't know if it's true, about a girl my age who ran away from her home in the States and came to Israel. She wrote a note and stuck it in the Wall and someone found it. The note said, "I'm lost" and had the phone number of her parents, and they had a reunion right here at the Wall. Is that true?

MAN: Makes you wonder why she didn't just send the note directly to her parents.

         Beat.

SARA: That's not the point.

MAN: So what is the point? *(Beat.)* Is the point that this place is special?

SARA: Yes.

MAN: Worth the trip from Canada?

SARA: Of course.

MAN: And more than that.

SARA: I guess.

MAN: You guess? Such a special connection? How much is it worth?

SARA: A lot.

MAN: Worth defending?

SARA: Yes.

MAN: Worth dying for? Worth killing for? Come on. Our direct phone line to God. *(Takes out a lighter and sets the prayer on fire.)*

SARA: What are you doing?

MAN: Do you think God didn't hear that prayer? Do you think He didn't get it, the minute that you thought it, before you even wrote it down? What makes you think you should come here, all the way from Canada, where apparently you can't pray, and limit God to this one place? You think God is so small? God is everywhere. Everywhere. He is here, and there, and there. You go home to Canada and you tell your Rabbi Bergman that. You tell him that Abraham broke the idols for a reason. We don't idol worship in Judaism, we don't worship a bunch of rocks, no matter how old. We worship God. Period. *(He starts to exit.)*

SARA: I want to be Christian. *(Gets on her knees and prays.)* Hail Mary full of grace, in kingdom come, thy will be done...and something about bread. No wonder Christians are so popular, they pray about bread. Not us. Oh no. We starve ourselves once a year so that we can pray better. If you're not allowed to eat, the rabbi says, you won't be thinking about food. What kind of logic is that?

HISHAM: The same logic that says "Security for Peace."

SARA: I would like to pray.

HISHAM: The same logic that says the world will be a safer place once we have control.

SARA: I would like to believe in something.

HISHAM: Typically Western logic.

SARA: Typically Palestinian logic to turn someone's personal spiritual crisis into something about the Occupied Territories.

HISHAM: Forgive me, but your personal spiritual crisis—

SARA: No, I know. I know. It's irrelevant.

HISHAM: Sara, listen to me—

SARA: It's funny how it affects me, though—

HISHAM: A Land With No People. For a People With No
                 Land. Oh yes, my grandfather left his home of
                 eight hundred years by choice. The land was really
                 empty anyway. My mother would be glad to see
                 her sons grow up to be murderers, terrorists,
                 because she's not a natural mother. You want to
                 talk about terrorism? You are standing in my
                 house. Your story takes place in my house. It is my
                 story.

SARA: I knew it. I knew it would come to this.

HISHAM: You have power now, Sara.

SARA: I just don't want to erase—

HISHAM: (Overlap.) You won the war. You have to accept
                 that.

SARA: You seem to want to erase. The beauty of what they
                 did, my ancestors, coming in boats—with nothing.
                 They built that country with nothing. Six million
                 dead and they did it. And I know that it's
                 complicated—it's a country you know—it's not an
                 idea—in people's heads, people like me, who have
                 no right to criticize—just because we're
                 disappointed—we're injured somehow because
                 we wanted it to be a light—something more—and
                 it isn't. It's just a country.

HISHAM: Sara. Where are the Palestinians in your story?

SARA: There aren't any.

HISHAM: This isn't just a conversation between you and
                 your Jewishness. OTHER PEOPLE ARE
                 INVOLVED.

SARA: Don't yell at me.

HISHAM: I WILL YELL AT YOU. I AM TIRED OF

CODDLING JEWS. I AM TIRED OF CATERING
TO YOUR DELICATE LITTLE EGOS. I AM
SORRY IF YOU ARE HAVING AN IDENTITY
CRISIS, BUT MY PEOPLE ARE DYING. THEY
ARE BEING CRUSHED BY YOU AND YOUR
FUCKING IGNORANCE. YOU THINK YOU ARE
STILL THE VICTIMS? THE PALESTINIANS ARE
THE VICTIMS OF THE VICTIMS.

Beat.

SARA: OK. You want to play a Palestinian? OK. It'll help
actually. It'll speed things up. I need something.
Here. *(She gets a balaclava and dresses him up as a
terrorist.)* Perfect. Just stand there, and don't say
anything.

"OK, Marnie. Let's finish the story.

Marnie wants me to apologize for the fact that.
(Beat.) That night at Dizengoff Square. That night,
she and I agreed to meet on Friday night in
Jerusalem. I promised to call her and confirm the
plan. But I never called. So she never came. "I want
you to know that I kept that plan. I sat and waited
for you for two hours on Ben Yehuda Street, and
then by some fluke I saw one of the girls on your
trip. She said that you'd decided to stay in Tel Aviv
for the day." She said that Marnie decided to stay
in Tel Aviv for the day. Then a boy ran up to my
table with a short wave radio and the BBC reports
started coming out: Seventeen-year-old girl from
Canada killed on a Tel Aviv beach. Seventeen-
year-old girl from Toronto. From North York.
From Truman Road. Marnie and I lived on the
same street so my parents… *(Beat.)* My parents
walked to her parents' house.

"The beach was crowded that day but only you
were killed. That man walked up and down the
beach ten times before he put the bag beside you.

He chose you. Why, Marn? I went to Rabbi Bergman, I went to the synagogue to ask that question, and he said, 'Why does God allow His Chosen People to suffer? Maybe so we'll never forget.' 'Forget what, Rabbi?' 'Forget who we are.' 'Who are we, Rabbi?' 'The Chosen People.' 'Chosen for what, Rabbi? Chosen for what?' *(Beat.)*

I don't know why I keep telling this story. I made a promise, Marn. I made a promise that I would never move beyond you. But I can't remember the point. And I'm tired. I just want to get on with it, you know? I'm sorry. I'm sorry. I am sorry.

> *Pause.*

She's gone.

> *Beat.*

And I don't even have to look at the clock to know that I'm thirty.

> *End of SARA's solo show. Sound of canned applause. SARA takes her bow and leaves. Spotlight on HISHAM, still in his balaclava. Applause grows louder, cheers, chants in Arabic "Death to Israel", etc. HISHAM raises his fist. Exultant, HISHAM takes off his mask. Silence.*

HISHAM: *(A la TV news anchor.)* AND LET'S GO NOW TO THE OCCUPIED TERRITORIES. According to the statistics documented by MIFTAH's Intifadah Report the number of Palestinian deaths is as follows 2044 in the West Bank 1991 in Gaza of the Palestinian civilians killed by Israeli troops 268 were women 866 were children 116 died because they were denied treatment or access to hospital of these 31 were Still. Births. Born dead at checkpoints TO CONTINUE 2,291,144 dunums of Palestinian land were confiscated 7703 Palestinian homes in the West Bank and east Jerusalem were completely destroyed or demolished 40, 415 Palestinians were left homeless but what is a home a home is a home is a home is where the heart is a home is a man's etcetera etcetera to continue A REPORT according to the Palestinian Environmental NGOs Network or PENGON on the Israeli Separation Wall or Isolation Wall or Colonial Wall or Apartheid Wall or as it is commonly called as the world knows it the SECURITY WALL begun in 2002 in spite of the advances of civilization in spite of the internet cable television the global village brotherhood of man in spite of the air the sky the water the land the land the land in spite of God and the Olympics and sports such as tennis in spite of the past in other words the facts to continue the facts the wall is the facts the facts just the facts ma'am approximately 8 metres high and may include some or all of the following concrete watchtowers trenches barbed wires cameras sensors and the soldiers oh the soldiers the soldiers TO CONTINUE the following on Palestinian land have been razed to the ground for the building of the Wall 102, 320 trees 14 km of roads 300 dunums of greenhouses 85 shops 7 homes and a partridge and a partridge and a PLAYGROUND. (*Takes a breath.*) In other words. Etcetera etcetera. To be brief. The past. In short the past. The past is a foreign country, as they say. A foreign country, as they say. In short...

> *SARA, as Leila, is dressed in a hijab. She speaks mostly in Arabic, but occasionally in English.*

LEILA: (Wake up, Hisham.)

HISHAM: ...the past is the past...

LEILA: (Hisham, wake up. Wake up, Hisham. Hisham—)

HISHAM: Why, wake up? I'm not asleep.

LEILA: (You are dreaming of Yafa again.)

HISHAM: I was not dreaming about Yafa.

LEILA: (Liar.)

HISHAM: Leila, please. Your place is by my side, not in my head.

LEILA: (Do you want to know where I am?)

HISHAM: I wish you would speak English.

LEILA: (I wish you would speak Arabic.)

HISHAM: Speaking Arabic will not help you learn English. How are we going to be world famous if you don't learn English? Nelson Mandela speaks English. Gandhi spoke English.

LEILA: (Do you want to know where I am?)

HISHAM: No. I don't want to know where you are. You are somewhere risking your life and I am not interested.

LEILA: (I am at a rally.)

HISHAM: A rally. What a surprise. Leila's at a rally. I think the shock will kill me.

LEILA: Stop joking and come to the university.

HISHAM: First of all, I will not stop joking because joking is what makes me so lovable. Second of all, I will not come to the university because I have no classes today and I do not wish to be an overly conscientious student.

LEILA: (You idiot. The rally is at the university. And it is big.)

LEILA: I am writing an article about it. Come on.

HISHAM: No, you come on. I tell you what, I am holding a rally right here in my bed and I invite you to join me. We will be John Lennon and Yoko Ono.

LEILA: (You are truly an idiot.)

HISHAM: I am not an idiot. I am a pacifist. I know the distinction is blurry but—

LEILA: (Sometimes you have to fight for peace.)

HISHAM: Fight for peace. Now that's a new one. Could you fight for peace *and* quiet? Shooting tends to keep me awake.

LEILA: (Listen to me, Hisham.)

HISHAM: *(Mumbling, half awake.)* Yes, yes, I'm listening.

LEILA: (LISTEN.)

HISHAM: Leila, don't shout like that. I am Editor of the University Paper. I deserve respect. You, on the other hand, are a lowly reporter—

LEILA: I AM GOING TO SHOUT SO LOUD.

HISHAM: I swear, I will retract, one by one, every proposal of marriage I've ever made you.

LEILA: (Today is the day, according to the Oslo Accord.)

HISHAM: What day according to the Oslo Accord?

LEILA: The day that we were to announce a Palestinian state.

HISHAM: Here, I'll make a toast. On May 4th, 1999, to the ALMOST Independent State of Palestine. Hey, it rhymes. Now is the glass half full or half empty?

LEILA: I want to tell this story.

HISHAM: So tell the story. Even better, take some pictures. If someone gets killed we might run it on page two.

LEILA: (Fine.)

HISHAM: Oh, so now you're mad at me for being a pacifist.

How like a woman. Do you think Dr. Martin Luther King Jr. had to put up with this from his wife? "I have a dream today!"

LEILA: (Enough, Hisham.)

HISHAM: "I have a dream that one day little Arab boys and Arab girls will ALMOST join hands with little Jewish boys and Jewish girls and ALMOST walk together as sisters and brothers."

LEILA: You are so angry, Hisham.

HISHAM: I am not angry. I am just losing my sense of humour. *(Beat.)* And now you are supposed to say, "You cannot lose what you never had," or something. Come on. *(Beat.)* OK. You win. For the rest of our lives you will always win. Describe to me what's going on at the rally and I will decide if it's worth the effort.

            Sound of shots being fired.

HISHAM: Leila? What's going on?

LEILA: (I have to go.)

HISHAM: No, don't go. Tell me what's going on.

LEILA: (I have to go, Hisham.)

            Lights down on Leila.

HISHAM: Leila! Don't do anything stupid! I am coming, OK? Wait for me there. Don't move! OK?

            Here I am, I am dressed and out the door in less than two minutes. I am on my bike, I am at the university, you are not where you said you would be and I DID NOT TAKE LONG, LEILA. Here I am, at the phone booth where you stood and phoned me and I am absolutely. Furious. I am going to shake you— WHERE ARE YOU—

Sound of shots being fired.

I am an idiot. I have climbed onto the roof of a nearby building which is stupid, really stupid. *(Sound of shots.)* AAAHH! *(Beat. Realizing.)* But no one shouts me. I look down the street, I see the rally moving in an orderly fashion, hundreds of Palestinian men maching peacefully hand in hand. In the centre of the crowd are eleven men in masks holding maschine guns. They pose for the cameras. CNN, NBC, CBS. *(Relieved.)* A photo op. Of course. Suddenly, the reporters scatter in all directions. The crowd has arrived at the checkpint and on the other side of the gate, I see the Israeli army waaiting. Leila. I see you. You are near the front of the crowd, nearest to the gate, with your camera ready. UP AGAINST THE WALL, LEILA. You idiot. You see? How suddenly alll the foreighn reporters have bullet proof vests and crash helmets? Where did they get them, you are wondering. I have been telling you this all along, Leila. We are performing for a larger audience. The Israelis vs. the Palestinians, watch them kill each other on your television set. You see that little boy, Leila? The one about to throw the Molotov cocktail? He will be on CNN tonight.

And now everthing is in slow motion. I see the boy run out into the street. I see you try to stop him. The gate slides back. Sound stops. The army comes out shooting. But I cannot hear. I see it, but I can't hear. I can't hear. I can't hear. I can't hear. I can't hear. I can't hear.

SARA: *(Overlap, to audience.)* I'm ready to apologize now.

HISHAM: I can't hear.

SARA: I'm ready to make peace. What we have here is an opportunity for two people to exist side by side. This is not an unsolvable conflict. This is not an eternal conflict. This an opportunity for hope. And all we need to seize this opportunity is a little good will, a lot of faith…and some chalk. *(She holds up chalk and proceeds to draw a line from stage left to right, dividing up and downstage, separating her from HISHAM.)* Do you see how much better that is? Already I can feel the tension easing. Don't you feel better Hisham?

Silence.

HISHAM: I lost a friend.

SARA: So did I.

HISHAM: Then you and I have to make peace. A real peace.

SARA: I don't know what to think…

HISHAM: I do not want to be a disappointed man, Sara. I can't—I grew up with… My father, my uncles, this look of—what?—*shame* in their eyes. The first intifadah—the one that killed your friend—I'm sorry but for those of us who were young, we were not ashamed. We were proud because we were fighting. And not only against the Isrealis but against everything, our own parents. For being so…beaten. But now I don't know what to think. I don't know. Help me. What hope is there if we can't—

SARA: Hisham.

HISHAM: Help me. Sara. Please.

Beat.

SARA: Come here.

HISHAM: What.

SARA: You heard me.

Beat. HISHAM looks down.

HISHAM: What about this line.

SARA: Just. Come here.

HISHAM: I do not come and go at your say-so, Sara. If you want me to come to you, then erase this line.

SARA: I can't believe this. You're negotiating?

HISHAM: That's right. Erase the line and we'll see what happens.

SARA: Don't do this. Can't yu see I'm trying—

HISHAM: Sara, believe me I want to come over there. But please understand that as a man—

SARA: What? As a man you're too pigheaded—

HISHAM: Sara.

SARA: Too stubborn—

HISHAM: You are the most frustrating woman I have ever met. If I were your husban I would...

SARA: You would what?

HISHAM: Erase this line, Sara.

SARA: Not on your life.

HISHAM: Erase it.

SARA: Make me.

They kiss. They look down at the line. Pause.

You know, I think you're right. Peace is overrated. It's like marriage. All the negotiations, all the compromises. You ask yourself, is it worth it? To have to smile when you want to spit. To cut your dick off, just so the other person doesn't feel threatened. To lie, and lie, and say everything's alright, when the truth is, you're dying, your soul is dying because of all those fucking compromises and you realize that you've traded freedom just to buy a little stability. And there's nothing stable about it, is there? It could fall apart at any time, and then it's like nothing ever happened. You're back to square one, only dickless. No thanks. I'm with you. Fuck peace. I want a divorce.

He picks up the chalk. HISHAM draws a line through the centre of the stage from up to downstage, dividing left from right.

SARA: What are you doing?

HISHAM: I am taking half the stage.

SARA: Not that way. That way.

Indicates upstage and downstage.

HISHAM: Oh, no.

SARA: I can't give you the front of the stage. I have to do my show.

HISHAM: What about my show?

SARA: You don't have a show.

HISHAM: Well, I am going to have one. And I can't do it all from back here.

SARA: OK. I tell you what, I'll give you stage right, if you give me all of downstage. *(Draws a line extreme downstage, from right to left.)*

HISHAM: That's completely unfair.

SARA: What are you talking about?

HISHAM: That is an insult.

SARA: Look, we're talking prime real estate here. I'm offering you the front of the stage.

HISHAM:	But that is not the front. That is the middle.
SARA:	The middle front.
HISHAM:	What is the middle front—
SARA:	OK, you drive a hard bargain. I can respect that. I'll give you the exact same section…but here… *(Draws a line extreme upstage, from right to left. The entire stage now looks like a tennis court.)*. So that way, it'll be equal.
HISHAM:	*(A whole lot of Arabic, some of it not very nice.)*
SARA:	Oh god, he's speaking Arabic again. Hisham, this offer is time-sensitive, so…
HISHAM:	*(To the audience.)* In your opinion, is this a fair way to divide the stage?
SARA:	Why are you asking them?
HISHAM:	Because they have been here since the beginning.
SARA:	What happened to "Art is not a democracy"?
HISHAM:	THIS IS DIFFERENT.
SARA:	Well, I'm against it. Them deciding. How do I know some of them aren't.
HISHAM:	What?
SARA:	Um…
HISHAM:	Oh, just say it.
SARA:	Anti-Semitic.
HISHAM:	I've got news for you.
SARA:	What.
HISHAM:	I'm Semitic too.

SARA: You know what? We need someone we can both agree on.

HISHAM: That will never happen.

SARA: A strong but silent type. A Solomon.

HISHAM: The one who suggested ripping the baby in half?

SARA: I've got an idea.

            She exits.

HISHAM: Can I have a show of hands for who thinks that dividing the stage this way *(Indicates left and right.)* is good and dividing the stage that way *(Indicates up and down.)* is a gross violation of my rights?

            SARA re-enters.

SARA: Can you help?

            HISHAM exits with SARA. They reenter, HISHAM carrying an A-frame ladder.

HISHAM: May I ask a question, please?

SARA: Put it over here.

HISHAM: Am I carrying the ladder because I am a man and I am strong or because I am brown and inferior?

SARA: Don't be ridiculous.

HISHAM: Just wondering if I am winning or losing.

            He sets the ladder down upstage centre.

SARA: There. Do you see that?

            He doesn't.

            The referee.

HISHAM: So we ask someone to sit up there?

SARA:	God, no. What would be the point of that?
	Beat.
HISHAM:	Sara. I am very. Tired.
SARA:	The referee enforces the rules, right? We already know the basic rules. Peace on Earth. Thou shalt not kill—
HISHAM:	Thou shalt not steal—
SARA:	Exactly. The referee is not important. The rules are.
HISHAM:	So he can be anything we want him to be?
SARA:	Yes, she can.
	Beat.
HISHAM:	I don't know.
SARA:	Have a little faith, Hisham. Shhh. *(She listens.)* You see? Right now, She's telling me that you were right. We should divide the stage this way *(Indicates right to left.)*.
HISHAM:	Really?
SARA:	Absolutely. With a few little adjustments. *(While speaking, she marks 'x' on three strategic sections.)* After all, She said, I really was here first. It was my show.
HISHAM:	I think He meant that you have dominated the space long enough.
SARA:	Sticks and stones, Hisham. There. Your areas are marked with an 'X'.
	Beat.
HISHAM:	Sara. How stupid do you think I am?
SARA:	That's what She said.

HISHAM: If you have these squares and this piece at the front and this at the back, how am I supposed to get to my territory? I will be stranded.

SARA: Walk on the lines.

HISHAM: This is ridiculous.

SARA: No, really. Any lines in your sections are yours, and any lines in my sections are mine. But the middle is no-man's land. Sound fair?

HISHAM: Oh yes, fair was exactly the word I was looking for. *(Beat.)* What about those *(Indicates table and chair centre stage.)*?

SARA: Those are mine.

HISHAM: No, they're not. They're in the middle.

SARA: I don't care. I paid for them, they're mine.

HISHAM: The referee doesn't think so. He says they're mine.

SARA: No, She doesn't!

            Both start to make their way to the table and chair as fast as possible, while trying to stay on their lines.

SARA: Hey—HEY! There is no way I am letting you—

HISHAM: I saw that! Your foot slipped. You forfeit the table.

SARA: You can't walk on the middle line. NO WALKING ON THE MIDDLE LINE!

HISHAM: Who died and made you—

SARA: I've got it! I've got the table!

HISHAM: So do I! I declare this table mine!

SARA: I already declared it mine at the store! Where I bought it!

Climbing and rolling over each other, they tussle for the table. Finally, exhausted, they give up. Pause. They try to catch their breath. Pause.

HISHAM: I am now officially at my lowest point.

SARA: That was fun.

HISHAM: Sara.

SARA: Hisham.

HISHAM: You are crazy.

SARA: Probably.

HISHAM: You mean we finally agree on something? I can't believe it.

SARA: Hisham.

HISHAM: Shhh.

                        Silence.

SARA: Hisham.

HISHAM: Sara. I can't talk anymore.

SARA: I'm hungry.

HISHAM: Mmhmmm.

SARA: I mean it, I'm starving.

HISHAM: Have a lemon.

SARA: Great.

HISHAM: Some garlic, tehine, chickpeas, a little pita bread. *(Beat.)* I miss my mother's hummous. If you are ever in Ramallah, you should stop by.

SARA: Oh sure.

HISHAM:	Palestinian hospitality. Doesn't matter if you are Arab or Jew, she will feed you.
SARA:	Hisham—
HISHAM:	Why do we hate each other? We are so much alike.
SARA:	I don't hate you.
HISHAM:	Our food is the same. Our mothers are the same.
SARA:	But could I live with you?
HISHAM:	You know, it's night time in Palestine right now.
SARA:	Hisham, you're tired.
HISHAM:	For Jews and Palestinians. Anyone who is looking up sees the same sky, the same moon.
SARA:	Let's not talk anymore.
HISHAM:	When I was a little boy, in the Jalazoun refugee camp, my grandfather would sit on my mattress and sing me to sleep. He had a terrible voice. And he would tell me stories of the days in Yafa when we had our own house with a lemon tree in the backyard. "That's what Yafa means in Hebrew," he would say. "'Beautiful'." And when I cried, he would say, "No, no, Hisham, you are the oldest, like me, and we must never cry. We must save our tears to water the lemon tree when we return home. Inshallah."
SARA:	Inshallah.
HISHAM:	You have a pretty voice. Better than my grandfather's.
SARA:	Thank you.
HISHAM:	Sara. Sara.
SARA:	What?

HISHAM: Nothing. Sing me that song.

SARA: Which one?

HISHAM: The one you did. Earlier.

SARA: I don't have candles.

HISHAM: Doesn't matter. Just sing.

She starts to sing the prayer over the candles. He listens to part of it, then joins in with the Muslim call to prayer. The prayers become increasingly competitive. Finally, SARA breaks off. Pause.

You see, I lost a friend.

SARA: So did I.

Pause. They have both moved into their own territories.

VOICE: *("Wimbledon" style.)* Quiet please. Quiet please. Quiet please. Thank you. And now let's go to the Middle East, where the score is love-all.

Sound of a serve. The sounds of a rally continue throughout, punctuating each report.

Israeli troops wound an eight-year-old boy and kill a Palestinian woman during a demonstration today in Hebron.

Palestinian militants kill pregnant Jewish settler and her four young daughters.

Israeli forces fire on Palestinian protesters in Gaza, killing ten.

Hamas bomb kills six Israeli soldiers and wounds three.

Israelis kill three, including man in wheelchair.

Five youths killed in clashes.

Four dead.

Three.

One.

The sounds of a rally continue, back and forth.

The End.